Baby Animals

RABBIT

Angela Royston

Chrysalis Children's Books

First published in the UK in 2004 by
Chrysalis Children's Books
An imprint of Chrysalis Books Group Plc
The Chrysalis Building, Bramley Road, London W10 6SP

Paperback edition first published in 2005

ISBN 1 84458 085 7 (hb)
ISBN 1 84458 494 1 (pb)

British Library Cataloguing in Publication Data
for this book is available from the British Library.

Editorial Manager: Joyce Bentley
Editor: Clare Lewis

Produced by Bender Richardson White
Project Editor: Lionel Bender
Designer: Ben White
Production: Kim Richardson
Picture Researcher: Cathy Stastny
Cover Make-up: Mike Pilley, Radius

Printed in China

10 9 8 7 6 5 4 3 2 1

Picture credits
Chrysalis Books/Jane Burton 19, 24.
Corbis Images Inc: Robert Pickett 4.
Ecoscene: Angela Hampton 9, 11.
Natural History Photo Agency: Michael Leach 5, 10, 14; Manfred Daneggar 22, 27.
Oxford Scientific Films: 13, 15; Scott Camazine 7.
Rex Features Ltd: 21.
RSPCA Photolibrary: William S Paton, cover , 2, 17, 18, 25; E A Janes 28; D Dedeurwaerdere 1, 29;
John Downer/Wild Images 20; Angela Hampton, 6, 8, 12; Tony Hamblin 16; Mark Hamblin 23, 26.

NOTE
In this book, we have used photos of both wild and pet rabbits. Pet rabbits usually have white, black or ginger-coloured fur and live in a hutch. Wild rabbits usually have brown fur and live in a burrow.

Contents

Just born

These baby rabbits have just been born. They have no **fur** and cannot see or hear. Their eyes are always closed.

Up to six baby rabbits are born at the same time. Some are pink and some are black.

One day old

The mother puts her babies in a **nest** she made inside a rabbit **hutch** or **burrow**.

The nest is made of **straw** and bits of fur. The baby rabbits sleep most of the time.

One week old

Each baby rabbit is now covered with soft fur.

These baby rabbits have white fur, but some have black, ginger or brown fur.

Feeding

The baby rabbits smell their mother's milk and crawl to her to find a **teat**.

Feeding makes them feel tired.
They soon go back to sleep.

Two weeks old

Now the baby rabbits have opened their eyes. They can see their mother and one another.

The baby rabbits can hear now, too. They hear noises inside and outside their hutch or burrow.

Three weeks old

The baby rabbits grow bigger and stronger every day. They crawl around inside their home.

A baby rabbit's **whiskers** help it to feel things. Its nose twitches when it smells something.

Exploring

Sometimes the baby rabbits go out of the hutch or burrow. Now they can **explore**.

They stay close to one another and do not go far from their home.

Grazing

The baby rabbits eat special rabbit food. They also like to **nibble** grass.

Rabbits also eat lettuce, apples and carrots. The more a baby rabbit eats, the bigger it grows!

Four weeks old

The baby rabbit's fur is growing longer and thicker.

The baby rabbits are growing fast, but they are still smaller than their mother.

Playing

The baby rabbits love to run around, jump and play.

Sometimes the baby rabbits pretend to fight. They do not hurt each other.

Eight weeks old

The baby rabbits are stronger and bolder now. They often play on their own.

The baby rabbits spend most of the day outdoors. They wander off far from their mother.

Watch out!

Rabbits must be careful. Birds like this one might attack them.

The mother rabbit squeaks to warn her babies of danger. They run quickly to the hutch or burrow.

Fully grown

The young rabbits are
six months old now and
fully grown.

This young mother rabbit is ready to have babies of her own.

Quiz

1 How many babies can a mother
rabbit have at a time?

2 How old are baby rabbits
when they begin to see and hear?

3 At what age does a baby rabbit first grow fur?

4 What does a rabbit use its whiskers for?

5 At what age do baby rabbits start to go outside?

6 What sound does a mother rabbit use as a warning?

7 What is a rabbit's home called?

8 At what age are rabbits fully grown?

The answers are all in this book!

New words

burrow underground home made in fields.

explore to find out for oneself.

fur thick hair that covers most of the body.

graze eat grass.

hutch special cage for rabbits.

nest a bed or home made by an animal.

nibble eat in small mouthfuls.

straw dried stems of cereal plants such as wheat and barley.

teat part of a mother's body from which her babies suck milk.

whiskers long hairs on each side of the face.

Index